Being Beautifully Strong

Mini Edition

Into your twenties and beyond

REBECCA DOROTHY VALASTRO

Copyright © 1996 Rebecca Dorothy Valastro
All rights reserved.
ISBN: 0-9954253-8-8
ISBN-13: 978-0-9954253-8-5
Published 2017

All rights reserved. No part of this book may be reproduced by any mechanical, photographic, or electronic process, or in the form of a phonographic recording; nor may it be stored in a retrieval system, transmitted, or otherwise be copied for public or private use-other than for "fair use" as brief quotations embodied in articles and reviews-without prior written permission of the publisher.

The author of this book does not dispense medical advice or prescribe the use of any technique as a form of treatment for physical, emotional, or medical problems without the advice of a physician, either directly or indirectly. The intent of the author is only to offer information of a general nature to help you in your quest for emotional and spiritual well-being. In the event you use any of the information in this book for yourself, which is your constitutional right, the author and the publisher assume no responsibility for your actions.

I've taken the best of the best!

Within this book, is 100 of my most favorite pages from Being Beautifully Strong: into your twenties and beyond.

This travel sized, bag size, easy to carry, read, borrow and lend size, is easy to have by your side every day of the year.

Be, see and feel amazing, because YOU deserve the very best and it's time you felt it every single day.

- from my heart to yours -
A piece of my inner strength.

B xxx

I can say NO to others and YES to me first.

No is not a bad word.

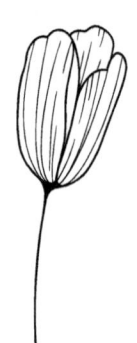

I Can Stand Strong.
And I do.

❝

If it doesn't feel good, don't do it.

Today I choose to feel good, because I am worth it.

Mistakes are just learning curves.
I can forgive me

I shine on the inside as much
as I shine on the outside.
As I shine, I brighten up
other people's day.

> I see myself as an extraordinary woman.
> I am kind and beautiful.
> I love what I see in me.

A new life is a new beginning. Being afraid to start over is totally normal. It's always hard when we first start out, like when we learnt to walk, took our first job, had our first heartbreak, became a mom.

If your heart is telling you to start a new job, find new friends, move house, leave a bad relationship... do you think you should listen? Your happiness is worth breaking through the initial fear, because a new beginning brings the possibility of new opportunities.

There is no rulebook to say
I cannot change my mind.
I can change my mind at
any moment and then
I can change it again.

Today I give myself permission to
make choices that are right for me.

To know peace, to feel love,
to be in harmony… sometimes we have
to experience the opposites; sadness,
grief, anger, greed. Those feelings
themselves aren't bad… but they are
linked to experiences that feel bad.
You can forgive yourself and move
into the feelings you deserve –those
of joy and happiness.

I remove judgment and I choose to see the benefit, the positive side. Even if it's not quite clear and the situation has created further challenges, I can choose to breathe and see the good... Seeing just one positive, one lesson learnt, one something that could generate some good, not only makes me feel better but helps me to deal with what needs to happen next.

I SHINE BRIGHT

In every sense of the word.

Brightly
Emanating Beauty
Kind
Loving
Beautiful Nature

That is me.

Being Beautifully Strong MINI

Just by being myself, I make others happy.

I Am Worthy of Great Love

YOU ARE AMAZING!

I truly mean that!

"

Let's be honest...

I am pretty AMAZING!

Did you laugh at that one?
I hope so... feels good to smile.

FYI... you are pretty amazing ☺

Every Day in Every Way

My Life gets Better & Better.

Embrace where you are right now. Here (as in this moment) is a result of your past thoughts and actions. The greatest part about this moment right now, is that you are creating the new of everything in your life from this moment forward. So don't sit in the past, repeating old thoughts constantly in your mind -it's already done.

Each moment is unfolding as the last one passes, so think amazing thoughts, see amazing things happening for you and each new moment will start to be more amazing and you will feel more amazing too.

Feeling is the key. When a thought feels good, it's doing me good. When a thought feels sad, whether it's someone else who did something to me or not, it only makes <u>me</u> feel bad... not them. They don't feel what I feel. So today I choose to feel good. I choose a positive thought or phrase to replace the negative ones.

Try and have a positive thought and make yourself feel bad at the same time — it's impossible. Make yourself feel good today, choose a positive thought instead.

If I feel pressured in a conversation, I can choose to respond with;

"Sounds great. Let me get back to you."

I can then go away and make choices that are right for me, without being convinced of doing what somebody else wants for me.

I am the only one in the world
who truly knows me.
People can say what they like,
but I know who I am.
I stay strong in my sense of being,
of what is true to me.

Every day I am my more perfect me.

66

I AM an Important Part of this World

> Sometimes things don't go to plan -don't stress. Sometimes it's because something better is at work, whether it's as complex as having your wheels clamped on your car and having to wait an hour for them to be removed and while you wait, you meet the man of your dreams and a year later you're getting married (true story, happened to my friend). Or maybe it's more simplistic, like you have to go back home for your wallet cause you left it on the bench and in doing so, you miss the five-car pile-up on the freeway. Sometimes the things that happen in our life are not just coincidences. Sometimes a greater force is guiding us, protecting us, leading us to the path that we should be on. Perhaps that's an angel, God or just your very own instincts. Whatever it is, instead of feeling angry when the instances occur, take a deep breath and say thank you. You never know the miracle that has just taken place... perhaps there was no miracle at all, but it sure does feel good to be grateful instead of angry.

Being Beautifully Strong MN

Time is on my side. I can take all the time I need to make the right choices for me.

A wise man once told me, "Hurt people, hurt people." Sounds cryptic? I didn't get it at first, but then I realized what he meant... someone who is happy and whole inside, would never need to hurt another, lash out at another, say a mean thing to another. Someone who is deeply in pain, will cause pain to others and not necessarily consciously do it. When we are in pain and we are hurting, it's hard to see the good, the positive. We act defensively, we may even harm others. I'm not making this behavior OK because it isn't, I just wanted you to know, that you can choose to let it go. You can choose to see that the person is in pain, that you are not the problem. A hurt person will hurt. You can choose to let them go, you can choose not to react, you can choose not to take their shit on. You are in control of you... and when you are hurting, remember these words, for no one is immune to the circle of causing and feelingh pain. Be the person who deals with her hurt, deals with her shit, so that what you pass onto others is love and compassion.

I take time to reflect on important decisions.

I haveven't always made the best decisions, but that doesn't mean I don't know how. If I listen to that inner voice, I know what is right for me. I am learning to trust myself with each day that passes.

I am truthful and honest
I am loving and giving
I am extremely kind
I am wonderful
I am amazing
I am full of potential
I am absolutely intelligent

I am ME!

I am loyal and brave, strong and open. Great things are coming to me every day.
I am loving to all and I'm allowed to be happy.

> Can you take a look at the map of the world. I want you to mark on that map a little red dot to indicate you. Then I want you to mark more little red dots on that world map that make up your family and friends. Then I want you to imagine how many other little red dots there are across the whole entire world. One little red dot for each person. When you do this, does it really matter what one person says about you? Or even what ten people say about you? They are just one dot in a sea of billions of dots across the whole entire world.
>
> You are special! There are billions of people out there that would think so too if they met you.

The more you focus on it, good or bad, your attention is creating it.

Focus on all the good currently in your life and then on the things you really want to happen in your life. When you focus on what you want, you begin to do what's necessary to make those things happen. When focusing on the absence of something, it demotivates you and stops you from taking the steps to get you where you want to be.

What are you focusing on today? Make sure it's something you actually want.

I am loyal & brave, strong & open.
Great things are coming to me
every day. I am loving to all and
I'm allowed to be happy.

I can change.
I can release my past.
I can release the hurt.

I ask for support.

It is there when I need it.

When you feel fear,
shift your attention to your
highest purpose. Imagine you
at your very best surrounded
by love & friendship.

I accept and love myself exactly
how I am right now.
I am a good, kind, loving
and caring person.

If you find yourself playing out scenarios in your head and they are making you feel really bad -try and end the scenario with an outcome that would make you happy instead. Think of the most positive, best outcome that you can imagine and then let that thought go.

Life can be really difficult when we are worried about what is happening in our lives OR more so, what MAY happen. Keep repeating this process -end the thought or image in your head with a positive outcome instead.

If you can possibly let it go, then that will help you to live in this moment with a little less stress in your head.

> Find the message in the fear you are feeling. Begin by acknowledging that the fear is there, then write down the specifics of what you are fearing. Can you turn that fear into humor, like the giant scary spider in Harry Potter that was given roller skates and couldn't stand up. Yeah it's real silly I know, but sometimes exaggerating the fear can help us to reduce the fear. For instance the fear of being lonely -if I make it as ridiculous as me living on an island with no books, no internet, no people, no music, no animals, no sun, no waves, no trees blowing in the wind; just absolutely nothing... well, by doing that, I can see that I am never truly alone. Helps me to appreciate what I do have around me.
>
> If you are experiencing life cripplingly fears, or fears that make you want to harm yourself or others, then please speak with a medical professional immediately. Your safety and happiness, as well as those around you, is the highest priority.

I will not compromise my dreams.
I am worth living all the possibilities
I have dreamed up for myself.
No one would ask me to compromise
my soul -that is where dreams come
from. Love doesn't stifle or drain,
nor does it ask me to give up that part
of me that makes me feel whole.
Our dreams are important.
We live one life... just the one.
It's meant to be lived in joy.

Not only do I have the ability to learn
new things and be a new person,
I have the intelligence and willpower to
perform any action that I desire.
I can be whoever I want to be. I can do
any job I choose to work toward.
I am more capable than anyone else
can see or imagine. I trust in me.
I will take me where I want to go.

Don't let anyone suck you into an argument. You choose anger. You are in control. Nasty words aren't worth the damage they do, nor the energy you waste. Your time is more valuable than that... and so are you.

I choose the windows of opportunity that are open to me. I move on from my past and I no longer tap on the doors that are closed. I see the beauty in a new day, which is full of new possibilities for me.

I live with passion and purpose.

No purpose is small or meaningless.
Purpose is what you live for.
Purpose uplifts others.
Like a mother whose purpose is to love and grow those special little human beings, or for the sales assistant to bring excellent customer service that puts joy into other people's day, or the nurse that eases the pain of a patient and the writer who writes in hope to inspire. Every single purpose is worth the passion you put into it.

Today I'm just gonna smile at everyone, because when I smile at the world, it generally smiles back. Even the people who are sad, lonely, having a bad day...
they may not smile back at me externally, but there is a tiny smile in their heart that makes them feel a little bit better inside.
You never know whose day you might change from simply giving them a smile. WE ALL have had days where we wanted to give up, we wanted to hide away, even days where we may not have wanted to wake up. When someone smiles at you or says a kind word, it can be the one thing that gets you to the next step. It can be the one thing that makes you choose to live.

Create your own Stars

If you can dream it,
you can make it happen!

Map it out, write it down.
Plan, take action and most importantly
believe. Don't give up. It takes time,
but our dreams are worth it.

I Am Capable!

When you visualize finishing your goal, you actually pave a way of how to finish the goal. If you can see yourself achieve it, then you certainly can find a way to get it done.

I AM a Strong, Supported, Loving Person.

Whatever happens, I can handle it. I have incredible strength within me.

I Feel Peaceful

On the days that I feel crazy, I sit and breathe. Calm slow breaths help me focus.

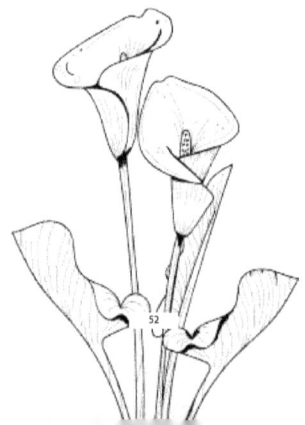

<u>Nothing</u> is Impossible
Only mathematically improbable.

I love this saying! I have no idea who said it, nor where it came from -it certainly isn't mine. I remember I was 15 years old when I started repeating this saying. I truly believed it. Life has been hard. It has really sucked at times. But I know true in my heart, that I can be, do and have, all that I want in this world. I just have to believe and do the work to achieve.

External events cannot destroy your dreams unless you allow them to. Let go of the illusion that you cannot change your life today.

Today I make the necessary changes that make me happy. Today I choose to live in Joy.

What would you do if you knew you couldn't fail, that success was guaranteed?

OK – now do it!

Fear of not being able to do something you love, is a waste of your precious heart.

Today I choose to believe in me.

❝

I ♡ My Body

I ♡ My Mind

I ♡ My Heart

I ♡ Being a Woman

I ♡ Being Me

❞

There are 3 steps to
accomplish great things:

Plan, Act, Believe.

I know you can do it.
I believe in you.
It's time you believe in you too.

I am Extraordinary

I have a very important job to do, being me ☺

I am Proud of me.

You've done an amazing job, being you.

I deserve to have every happiness in the world, in my life right now.

Yes you really do!

Today I make good choices for me.
I surround myself with people who
are kind like me.

Breathe.

When you feel yourself starting to panic, take 3 really slow long breaths in & out.

If it helps, count in for 6 and out for 6.

repeat:

I am Calm & Centered

Every day I am getting stronger & stronger.

It's not right for me to make others wrong, when we have walked in completely different shoes. No two lives are exactly the same. We all experience life differently.

I know wrong from right, but I don't make others wrong because I think that I am right.

Holding onto anger and onto the past, only hurts you. No one else knows what you are thinking or how badly it affected you. The person you hurt by constantly thinking about it, is you.

Today I forgive because it's the best thing I can do for myself.

Why am I angry with you?
Why do I need you to change?
Do I have an unfair expectation
of you? All valid questions only YOU
can answer. If you feel unhappy more
than you feel happy when you are
around a particular person, it is OK to
let them go. If we cannot accept people
the way they are, if all we want to do is
change them, then it is best we let them
go. You can never truly change another
person. They have to make that
choice for themselves.

Today I let others decide who they want
to be, just as I choose who I want to be.

People only factor in what they know, what they have read, what they have experienced.

Don't take anybody's word as gospel. People repeat what they heard from a friend, what they read on the Internet or saw on the news. These are just people's opinions. Don't feel as though you know nothing in comparison, or that you have to believe what they tell you either. Always investigate for yourself, because people will always give you advice whether they are an expert or not and whether you asked for it or not. There is a lot of mumbo jumbo out there –so don't take anything as truth, not even this book!

If it doesn't feel good, if it doesn't fit into your values, then don't do it, don't read it and make the choice for yourself and not because someone else told you, that you should or shouldn't believe it.

I trust in Me.
I know when to listen to Myself.
The funny feeling inside,
my instincts,
are letting me know when
something isn't right.

Today I relax knowing that I am a good person.

Never feel offended. People don't know you, like you know you, so who cares what they think about you. Nobody ever really has the full story. Unless they have lived your life, they don't really know your life.

Being Beautifully Strong MINI

Leaving a friendship, family member
or partner, especially with kids,
is difficult, scary and heartbreaking.
Chances are, you already know
the right thing to do.
You feel it in your heart.

Place your hand over your heart and
shut your eyes. This may seem silly,
but simply ask your heart what it
wants and what to do. It knows.
It won't deceive you.

I Trust my Heart

"

You don't have to stay anywhere that makes you feel unhappy. You are here to be loved, to celebrate and live life. If you find that you are sad and feel trapped, lean on people around you. If you are in an unsafe environment, please reach out and get professional support and help. There are so many of us across the globe that are here for each other, that want the best for one another. Never feel alone because you are not and if you feel afraid please let someone know, for no one should live in constant pain nor constant fear.

It is OK for me to reach out for support. If I cannot trust anyone close to me, then I can choose to call a helpline or even the police.

You can't really blame anyone else for the situation you are in. The job you hate, the marriage, the social event, even the abusive relationship. At some point you knew it was wrong. Whether we like to admit it or not, we ignore the instinct, that feeling inside telling us not to do it, take it, love it.

It's going to be OK. It takes years, sometimes a whole lifetime to listen to that inner voice... and not just listen to it (cause often we do hear it), but to trust it. To act on it. Knowing that you can make better choices for you, is the first step for change. It can be scary going into a new job or new relationship or even making a new decision after we've made choices that have hurt us, but acknowledging it, is the first step to trusting yourself again. It's the first step in seeing that you deserve more, that you are worth more. I truly believe it is your birthright to feel great -to be loved.

You deserve it and you should have it.

I forgive me.
　I've done my best in every moment.
　　I may not have been perfect,
　　　but nobody is. We all learn as we go.

Sometimes all you need to do to move forward is decide.

Make a choice.

We are often feeling stuck because we are too afraid to make one choice or another. Not making a choice <u>IS</u> making a choice. It's choosing to stay stuck in that moment.

I make clear decisions.

I make the right choices for me.

"

Write on a piece of paper or simply just think about all the things you have achieved. From shooting that goal in basketball as a kid, right up to getting your first job, going on that holiday and being blessed enough to have fallen in love. See all the work you have put into your life and feel inspired again. Your life is truly unique; as are you and the person you should be most proud of, is You.

"

I choose my destiny

-pick a good one that makes you happy-

Being Beautifully Strong MINI

I Am a Strong Confident Woman

“

I radiate beauty, health, love and kindness.

I shine like the brightest star!

”

"

I count. I matter.

I truly make a difference
in other people's lives.

Asking questions is the best thing in life. It will get you out of an awkward conversation or an uncomfortable job interview, it'll make you better at your job and you will know more about other people then you could ever have imagined. Never be afraid to ask. No question is stupid, regardless of what anyone might say. Sometimes people brush you off because they don't know how to answer it or because they don't know the answer. Continue to ask questions anyway, because being curious is a good thing.

Don't force it
Don't obsess
Let it go

That which is right for you, doesn't need to be forced. You are worth the best in life. Don't waste your time on those that don't see it or nurture it. You're just too special & too amazing to not feel joy in every moment.

Create your own fashion.

Let's be real... when you're dead, you won't give a crap, so wear what you want, when you want, how you want. You look fabulous always -it's just a matter of perspective... and trust me, only your perspective matters. So feel fabulous today in anything you wear.

> Whether people think this book is wish-washy or silly to do affirmations... I want you to know, you really do deserve the best in life.
>
> I deserve the very best in Life.
> I deserve to be Loved.

I let conversation flow.

You never know what you might learn by really listening to others.

You know you can be whoever
you want to be.
-reinvent yourself today-
Be whatever, whoever, however
you want to be.

One Life – Be Bold

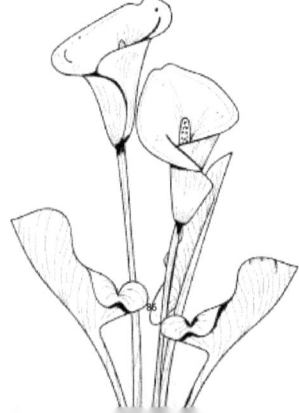

"

Perseverance
Perseverance
Perseverance

I Never Give Up!

Persist
Pursue
Endure

-no one can believe for you-

Stay focused. Get it done.
Give it everything you've got,
every second, of every day.

-it's worth it!

Stop thinking about it.
Put your Plan into Action.

I Am Focused
I Take Action Now.

"

Have you seen the movie Pollyanna? I feel like this was the message from that movie: if you are constantly negative, you put yourself in misery and you push out all the good in your life. When you start to focus on one small positive thing, you begin to feel good and it has a knock-on effect on those who surround you. Of course it is your right to be sad when you are going through a tough time, but ask yourself - how long has this tough time been weighing me down? Isn't it time you felt good? I know sometimes affirmations can feel stupid and not real... but it's a start. As you begin to feel more joy, pick 5 things you are thankful for and every morning really feel how grateful you are for those 5 things. You'll be amazed at how much better you can feel by simply shifting your attention to something that generates good feelings. I apologize for saying "simple" - I know it's not. But the more you do it, the more simple it becomes and the more you feel good too.

Please speak to a medical professional if you feel down all the time. They can help you.

"

I Feel at Peace with Myself & Others.

> I am a calm, confident, centered, powerful, strong woman. I receive all that I ask for. I am the luckiest girl in the world. Love, success, fortune, are abundant in my life. I am incredibly talented. I am excited and full of life. The more love and energy I give, the more love and energy I have to give. I am passionate, loving, caring and kind. I am compassionate. I am sexy, I am stunning, I am incredibly intelligent, I am amazing, I am extraordinary. I have a gorgeous face and body. I have beautiful hair and vibrant youthful skin. I live an amazing fantastic fun life, which I love and I am very grateful for it. I love every day. I love every moment. I love this moment. Thank you! I love all people exactly as they are. I am always smiling. People feel loved by me and comfortable around me. I bring people love and laughter. I am charismatic! Nothing is impossible. I am motivated. I am inspired. I am full of joy and I bring joy to others. I have great love in my life. I am greatly loved. I am surrounded by people who love and care about me and want the best for me. I am a strong and worthy woman.

> I am excited about life!
> My life can change
> and get better,
> at ANY second
> of any DAY!

It is in your past with others,
that you can find forgiveness.
It's in your past together, because
of the moments you shared
together, that you can forgive.
Think of a really happy moment,
a long time ago, a special moment,
a moment of love or laughter.
It is from there that you
can forgive.

I deserve to be loved with absolute
passion and commitment. I deserve
to be treated with respect and asked
if I am OK. What I deserve is
exactly what I put forward.
I deserve all the wonderful things
that I can see for me.

When you stay in an abusive relationship, whether it's a friend, family member or partner, you are showing yourself how little you are worth. The thing is, you are worth **THE WORLD**.

You are amazing and wonderful, beautiful and strong. You are kind and caring and giving too. You deserve the most precious life, full of laughter and fun. You are worth so much more.

My RSVP for the rest of the year...

"I'm Busy"

If you have a massive dream, an important goal, it's up to you to decide where your time is better spent -in endeavors that make you happy rather than with people who make you feel less? You are influenced by those who surround you. Choose wisely.

Today I choose to see how wonderful I truly am and that I am worth living the greatest life.

Today I Live in Joy.

Today I choose to see that I am lovable, that I am worth being loved. Today I Live in Love.

Don't be afraid to work hard for what you want. It is your choice. If you want something for your life, you can choose to work hard for it.

Work is my choice!

I choose it wisely.

"

Don't be afraid to believe in Miracles.

They happen.

You need to be 100% for
you as well as for others.
Look after yourself.

I AM

Healthy Rested Energized

Got a big job, career or dream and your family or friends aren't supportive...

"I could cry about just how unsupportive they are, OR I can just get on with the job and support myself."

I am not going to begin explaining particles, subatomic particles, atoms nor nuclei (I'm clearly no scientist but I read). What is suggested, is that we are all made up of energy. Everything is. When you get down to the very core, everything is energy. So if particles move and vibrate to form matter, and the particles at the very core are made up of energy, then we can change energy, which we do with our thoughts and feelings and feelings are determined by our thoughts. So basically we really are only limited by our thinking!

That was my fun fact ☺ but don't take my word for it, read about it yourself.

Always remember what I said earlier; don't take anything you read or hear as gospel truth, investigate for yourself. That's the only way you'll know for sure!

We learn and grow. Don't ever be embarrassed about the shit you have been through. Share it with others so that they may learn without having to suffer through it as you did.

Let's take care of each other.

We all can.
So let's choose to.

Being Beautifully Strong MINI

www.ingramcontent.com/pod-product-compliance
Lightning Source LLC
Chambersburg PA
CBHW052131010526
44113CB00034B/1768